This book may be returned to any Wiltshire
library. To renew this book phone your library
or visit the website: www.wiltshire.gov.uk

Wiltshire Council
Where everybody matters

LM6.108.5

Splitting the Arrow

Understanding the Business of Life

Prem Rawat

文屋
bun ya
Japan

Deep in the mountains lived a gardener. Every day he would walk down to the stream that ran through the valley and fill two clay pots with water for his garden.

With the pots full and balanced on either end of a wooden pole, he would carry them up the steep path that led to his garden high on the hillside. This was arduous work, but the man took great pleasure in looking after his garden. One hot summer's day, half way up the path, he decided to take a rest. When he lay the pots down, a small rock sticking out of the ground made a little hole in one of the pots.

A few months later, while the gardener was taking a nap down by the stream, the pot without a hole said to the other, 'You are useless.'

The pot with the hole replied, 'What do you mean I am useless?'

'You have a hole in you. Every day our owner works so hard to carry the water to his garden, but by the time we get there most of your water has already leaked out.'

On hearing this the pot with the hole became sad.

The next day the pot told the gardener how he felt.

'Tell me my friend, why are you so sad?' replied the gardener.

'Every day you fill me with water and work so hard to climb up the mountain, but by the time we reach the garden most of the water has leaked out.'

'This is true. You have a hole,' said the gardener. 'But do you know what that means?'

'It means I am useless. I can no longer fulfil my task which is to contain the water,' said the pot, feeling even sadder.

'Have you looked at the path we walk up to reach the garden?' asked the gardener. 'Thanks to you, the side of the path is full of flowers. When I realised you had a hole I started planting seeds along the path. Now the path is adorned with beautiful colours, and bees come to gather nectar from those flowers. You see, you are not useless at all.'

You

Do you know who you are?
That may sound like a strange question,
but your story truly begins when you can start
to feel what is happening inside you.

If this life is your story, wouldn't you want to make sure it is an interesting one?

Some people want their story to be an adventure. They want to climb the Himalayas or do things no one has ever done. But the greatest adventure is looking within and getting to know the real you, the one that never changes, even as your body ages.

You will be with you all through this story, but will you befriend yourself? Are you willing to listen to what you really want? Something that you have always wanted, a want that will not go away. When you can feel that, you are ready to write your story.

You know about the people around you,
but do you know yourself?

03

Patient: Doctor, I am in pain.

Doctor: Where does it hurt?

Patient: It hurts everywhere. When I touch my head it hurts. When I touch my jaw it hurts. My ear, my leg — everywhere it hurts.

Doctor: I see. I think your finger is broken.

04

Have you worked on your relationship with you? Or have you been more concerned with what other people think of you?

We worry about how our neighbours and colleagues see us. We have learned to measure ourselves with the scales of the world, to measure our status, our level of success.

What is important is how we feel about us. Do we feel good, do we feel at ease, or not?

Don't waste a moment measuring yourself. Begin to lend your ear to what is happening inside you. Get to know that companion, that strength.

The coconut

Whenever you see a tiny, uninhabited tropical island, you will see a coconut tree there, standing tall. How did it get there? It made an unlikely journey through a truly hostile environment. It doesn't have a map or a GPS, nor does it have a sail or an engine, but that little coconut contains within it everything it needs to make its journey. Water is required to stay alive in the ocean and to sprout when the coconut gets to the new shore. On its journey it will be surrounded by water, but it can't use that salt water, so the coconut packs its own sweet water. The coconut's husk provides flotation and protection throughout the journey and it sticks out of the water just enough to catch the wind and act like a sail.

With great courage the coconut sets off for an unknown destination. Falling from the tree, it gets bounced around in the surf. Again and again it tries to get out into the open ocean, and once it does, it starts catching the wind, catching the ocean currents and it is on its way. In the middle of this vast ocean, with huge waves, the little coconut shows no fear. We build ships, huge tankers, but when the storms come, those ships head to the nearest port until the storm passes. Not the humble coconut. With each wave it goes up and with each wave it will tumble down. That storm has been harnessed into something that helps it on its way.

Then one day with a high tide it gets washed up onto a new shore. Quietly it puts down its roots and in time another coconut will one day be ready to set sail from there. The coconut makes the most of what it has, it grabs each opportunity without hesitation and it finds its niche. The place where it can be.

We also have the essentials we need in order to find our niche. To make use of our courage and find a place within us where we can be at ease with ourselves.

Choice

With clarity make a choice,
then put it into practice.
Develop your ability to feel what is going on within you
and let that be your foundation in life.

Believing is a bit like standing in a line where you never quite get to the counter. There are lots of other people in the line and everybody is waiting for something special to happen when they finally get to the front. Waiting for someone special to appear and solve their problems.

You are the most qualified person to solve your problems. If you can start to see clearly, make good choices and turn those choices into actions, you will have no need to believe in something that may or may not actually happen.

In life we must make choices. Even when we find ourselves in desperate situations, we still have to make choices. Sometimes that can be hard, but each one of us has a source of great strength within. When we don't know of that strength, we search for someone to help us. But there is no need to search outside, when you have an incredible strength within. All you need to do is connect with it.

I have seen people at rock bottom, in the most difficult circumstances you can imagine. I go to prisons and speak to people who have no chance of ever leaving those confines. No privacy. Always a threat of violence in the air. Dire circumstances. Yet I have seen those same people find a strength within themselves and begin to shine. Not a fantasy, not a nice idea, but in reality.

Make use of your strength, make use of your sincerity and get to know the real you, the inner self. Then, with that strong foundation, make choices and start to practically apply that which you have chosen.

The two ants

One day two ants happened to cross paths.

One ant lived on a sugar hill and one on a salt hill.

'I haven't seen you around here before, where are you from?' said the salt ant.

'I live on the sugar hill,' replied the sugar ant.

'Sugar hill? What's sugar?' inquired the salt ant.

'Sugar is delicious and sweet. Just thinking about it makes my mouth water. Are you sure you've never eaten sugar before?'

'All we have around here is salt. You can eat it, but it makes you very thirsty. I like the sound of this sugar you speak of.'

'Well then, come and visit my sugar hill and see for yourself how good it tastes.'

The two ants set a date and decided to meet at the sugar hill.

The sugar ant gave directions how to get there.

As the day of the visit approached, the salt ant started to think.

'What if I don't like the sugar? I would have travelled such a long way and I will be hungry. Just in case, I'll take some salt with me in my mouth.'

At the sugar hill, the sugar ant was waiting to greet the salt ant.

'Welcome to my sugar hill. Here, try some sugar and see how good it tastes.'

The salt ant put some sugar into his mouth. 'Hmmm, this tastes just like my salt,' he said.

Puzzled by this response, the sugar ant said, 'Are you sure? Sugar and salt taste very different. Try some more.'

The salt ant put some more sugar in his mouth and after a moment said,

'Yep, this is the same taste as my salt. Around here you call it sugar, but where I live we call it salt. It's the same thing.'

The sugar ant knew that salt and sugar tasted different, so he knew something was wrong. He thought for a while and then said, 'Open your mouth so I can see what's in there.'

When the salt ant opened his mouth, sure enough there was a big lump of salt.

'There is the problem. Take out that salt and then taste the sugar again,' said the sugar ant.

The salt ant took out the lump of salt and tasted the sugar.

He finally got to taste the sweetness. 'Wow, this is incredible! So sweet. I'm never going back to my salt hill,' he said.

In life we have to leave one step behind in order to take the next. Success is built on our ability to evolve, to learn and to grow. To evolve, we must take along what's good, and leave behind what isn't needed.

The more we can do this, the more successful we will be. This story also shows how, at times, we are our own worst enemy. We have a tendency to not accept things as they are and to see everything through our own filters.

Some people ask me, 'Do I even have a choice? Isn't all this determined by the movements of the stars?' As if the cards have already been dealt and you are not the one making the decisions.

The answer I give is, 'No, it's not the stars.' Our own confusion is what leads to bad choices, and that is what creates most of our problems. When we can let go of our ideas about how things should be, we can start to see things as they are. Then we have the full range of choice.

When we can start to make conscious choices, it is like a lamp being lit.

When a lamp is lit, no matter how small that lamp, we can see things we couldn't see in the darkness. Making con-scious choices becomes your strength, your own lamp that gets rid of darkness.

The world is full of problems, yet there is also a lot of joy. There may be a thick layer of grey cloud, but just above that cloud is a magnificent, clear blue sky and the sun is shining. The question is, where do you want to be? It is your choice.

The learned parrots

There was a man who loved to raise parrots. One day he decided he would raise the most learned parrots, so he bought two parrot eggs. He kept them in a warm place and they hatched into chicks. As he took care of them he began to teach them everything he knew. He taught them science and history, and played music for them. As they grew they went on to learn more and more complex things and by the time they were adults they had learnt a lot. They could recite Beethoven's symphonies perfectly. They had memorised Newton's laws of physics and all kinds of complex formulas.

One day the man passed away, leaving the two parrots alone in the house.

When the relatives came to tidy up the man's belongings, they found the parrots. Nobody wanted to take care of them, so they put the cage by the window and opened the door. The two learned parrots hopped out onto the branch of a tree just outside the window. They climbed up to a higher branch where a wild parrot was sitting, and they struck up a conversation.

'We are very learned parrots. We know about science and literature and music,' they said.

The wild parrot was clearly impressed, so they continued to show off their talents, reciting poems and formulas.

As this continued, the wild parrot began to look at the learned parrots with awe. They had learnt so much while he knew so little.

While the learned parrots were reciting a symphony, out of the corner of his eye the wild parrot noticed a cat at the bottom of the tree. It had seen them and was starting to climb up the trunk. The wild parrot asked the two learned parrots, 'Do you know how to fly?'

'Of course we do. The air pressure below the wing is greater than the pressure above. This allows us to fly,' they said.

'No, no, not the theory. I mean can you actually fly?' said the wild parrot.

'No. But we know so much. Surely not knowing that one little thing doesn't matter,' replied the two parrots.

The wild parrot stretched out his wings and took off from the branch. As he did, he said to the two learned parrots, 'You really are learned, but the one thing you really need to know, you don't. Good luck.'

Remember when you were learning to ride a bicycle?

'Pedal, pedal, pedal, look straight ahead and keep your balance.' Someone who was trying to teach you probably gave you this advice, but even if you remembered it, the result was always a fall. Again and again you fell. Then one day, you got it. You felt the point of balance. Once you feel that balance you know how to ride a bicycle with or without the formula.

The story of the parrots and the example of the bicycle show the difference between academic information and practical knowledge. In the age we live in, information abounds. More people have graduated from universities than ever before. Yet this has not helped us solve the global issues we face. Things just seem to get more and more complex and problematic.

Information is important, but for the essential things in life, you need to know. You need to feel, to make it real for you, so that you can practically apply it in your life.

Growth is like being on a large sailboat. You start off on the deck and from there you can see a certain amount. If you climb up the rigging a little, you can see that much more. Then, if you go a little higher, you can see further still. If you keep climbing you will get to the crow's nest right at the top. From there you can see everything around the boat and for quite a long way. Growth is not a process of creating new scenery, it is a process in which you get to see things clearly, to see things as they are.

Peace

There are three levels at which conflicts take place.
The first is between two countries.
The second is between two people.
The third is the conflict that rages within an individual.
The conflict within an individual will lead to conflict
between people, and conflict between people will lead to
conflict between nations.

The wars we see in the world and the disagreements we have with those around us all start within human beings. The external wars can be temporarily ceased, but unless the conflict taking place within individuals is resolved, sooner or later it will re-ignite the external conflicts.

The first step is for individuals to nurture and practise peace within their own hearts. When enough individuals can do this, then the external wars can come to an end.

Finding peace is not about climbing high mountains and becoming someone who feels and expresses no emotions. It is simply a question of looking within oneself. Real peace that you can experience does not exist somewhere else. It is inside you.

15

Have you made peace with yourself?

The tortoises' picnic

One day a family of tortoises went for a picnic. They prepared the food and drinks and a blanket to sit on, and packed it all into their picnic box. They set off and walked along, searching for an ideal spot to have their picnic.

Being tortoises they walked slowly and so it took them a while to find the perfect spot.

Once they had their spot, they went about setting up the picnic, laying down their blanket, unpacking the sandwiches and drinks.

'Oh no, I forgot the bottle opener,' said the mother tortoise.

'Go back and get it for me, will you, dear?' she said to her eldest boy.

'I'm not going back to get it!' the boy cried.

'Why not?' she said.

'If I go, he will eat my sandwich,' he said, pointing at his younger brother.

'I promise he won't eat your sandwich,' said the mother in a reassuring tone.

This discussion went on for some time, until eventually the eldest son agreed to go back to get the bottle opener. Then he set off for home.

One week passed and the younger brother tortoise started to get hungry.

'Do you think my brother will really come back? I am hungry and I would like to eat that sandwich,' he said, pointing at his brother's sandwich.

'Let's wait a little more,' said the mother.

Two days later the younger brother was famished, and he asked again, 'I am starving. Can I eat that sandwich now?'

'Well, your brother has been gone a long time. Go ahead and eat it son,' said the father.

So the younger brother picked up the sandwich and just as he was about to take a bite, the elder brother popped out from behind a tree, where he had been hiding the whole time.

'I knew it! I knew you were going to eat my sandwich!'

This is the state of the world today. Between people, between nations there is so much distrust, so much removing of each other's dignity. Rather than get on with what needs to be done, people are watching each other out of distrust.

Rather than joining forces to tackle the real issues humanity is facing, we are busy pointing fingers at each other.

The reasons and systems of human beings have become more important than the humanity itself.

I have spent my life pointing to the peace inside us, the peace we need to feel, because that is the one missing element.

We are good at everything else. We have sent a rocket to the moon, we have made tiny mobile phones, we have removed money and can buy things with little plastic cards. So much progress in technology, but the peace inside us and human dignity are not progressing. We all need to develop our own inner understanding and then do whatever we can to increase the conscious awareness of humanity, so we can come together and tackle the issues that face us.

As a small baby, when you had a need you cried out, when you were content you smiled.

Your fundamentals have not changed since then.

Start to become aware of the need you have to be fulfilled.

When you can acknowledge that need, you have taken the first step towards making it a reality in your life.

You invest a lot of energy in being comfortable. So you can feel comfortable at night you buy a nice bed. When you buy shoes you try them on and take a little walk around the shop to make sure they fit properly. This is an effort we all make in order to keep our bodies comfortable.

Do we also invest in being comfortable within ourselves?

Or do we just get used to feeling empty inside? To feeling confusion? To feeling anger?

Do we get used to coping rather than flourishing?

That would be like trying on shoes that have a big nail sticking up through the sole and saying, 'These shoes will do fine.'

When we touch something hot, our body is hardwired to pull our hand away. It is a protective instinct we all have.

Do we not also have an instinct that pushes us to feel comfortable within?

If it comes naturally to you to want to feel good inside, then you should make it happen.

Within us is a garden. A garden that is not affected by the confusion in the outside world. A garden that no one can come and disturb.

In the world around us there is love and hate, there is suspense and mystery. The daily drama is unfolding.

However, there is a place inside you where you can be as you are. No pretences, no lies. A place where you can be completely at ease.

Such a garden exists inside everyone.

Put aside the titles and roles you play every day. In that inner garden you can be with you, just you.

Even if your freedom were taken away and something terrible were to happen to you, nothing can take away the most precious thing that you carry within you.

It is your choice whether you make an effort to get to know that which is within you.

Maybe in your life you will come to a point where you think, 'That's it, it's over for me.'

In that moment remember that the most important thing is still inside you and always will be. What you carry within is truly yours.

Life

What are you living for?
For the yesterday
that will never return?
Or for the tomorrow
that will never arrive?
The only place you can be
is the moment called *now*.

25,550 days

The average lifespan is 70 years.
That's 25,550 days.
How will you spend this one?

How many times a day do we look at a clock?

Do we understand what that clock is saying to us?

It is telling us we won't be here forever.

Time only moves in one direction, and when our time is up there is no way to extend it.

What does that mean for you?

A tree does not look at a calendar.

Trees don't say to each other, 'Tomorrow is the first day of spring, let's celebrate. Are you ready to bloom?'

The tree just follows the natural cycle of the seasons as they come and go.

In your life also, the spring should come, you should bloom and celebrate that you are alive today.

When the season comes, the tree will bloom, and when your season comes, take that opportunity.

Live this moment

We often hear that life is a gift.

Sometimes we struggle to see it that way.

We hear that life is precious. But in the busy routine of every-day life we often forget.

Every day the alarm clock goes off and our routine begins. In our minds we know what we need to do.

'I must go to the bus stop, I must get to the train, I must get to my office on time.'

All these musts that we place in front of life itself.

Some people are in a hurry. 'Faster, faster!'

Why are you hurrying? Don't you know what is waiting at the end of this journey?

Time is an interesting thing. Sometimes it goes by slowly, sometimes it goes by quickly. But it doesn't let you go any slower than it, or any faster. You are caught on this little boat, and it makes its passage down this river in its own time. The purpose of this life is not to get to the end; it is *now*.

It is to feel what is within.

It is to enjoy every fractional moment.

Live this moment, every moment.

If you want to understand why you are alive,
centre yourself in the moment called *now*.
Your life, being fulfilled, you existing –
these things all reside in the now.

When you think you have reached a dead end in your life, turn around and head back. Let that be the start of a new road. If you can live your life like that, every day can be fulfilling. Even when things look hopeless, you can find something beautiful in that day.

Your actions have produced the results
you see in your life right now.
If you don't like the results
you need a new course of action.

The king's desserts

The king summoned his chef. 'Today,' he said, 'I want you to make the most delicious dessert for me.' The chef nodded and went back to the kitchen.

This may not seem an unreasonable request, but it is what happened every day. The king wanted the most delicious dessert every night. And the routine was starting to wear thin for the chef. Every evening the king had his dinner, and no matter what the chef conjured up, the king was not satisfied. 'The most delicious dessert' is all the chef heard, night after night.

Well, today he was going to do something about it and give the king something to remember.

And remember it the king did! After dinner, the most sumptuous dessert was brought in front of the king. The aroma filled the palace.

Everyone who smelled it felt their mouths beginning to water. Tonight the chef had outdone himself.

As the king began to feast on the dessert, he noticed that mice from all around the palace had been drawn into the royal dining room by the wonderful smell. They were everywhere. The dining table began to fill up with mice. They were crawling on the curtains and not even the king's beard was spared as the mice searched for any tiny morsel of the leftover dessert.

This was a royal disaster. Mice everywhere – on the carpet, over the paintings and tapestries – and more were still coming.

An emergency meeting had to be convened to ascertain how to deal with the problem.

Clearing his throat the king said, 'What will we do? We have been invaded by mice. Speak up if anyone has any ideas.'

The ministers talked among themselves and declared, 'Your Royal Highness, we have come to the conclusion that cats

should be called in to clear the mice.'

Now this seemed reasonable.

The general was summoned and given orders that all the cats in the kingdom were to be collected and brought to the palace immediately.

Soon the cats started to appear and this did indeed get rid of the mice, but now the palace was full of cats.

Cats, cats, everywhere! Scratching everything, lounging on the royal furniture, sharpening their claws on the royal curtains. The constant miaows and purrs were almost deafening.

It was time for another meeting.

The king started off, 'Well, any more ideas?'

As before the ministers got into a loud argument. After some time they declared, 'Your Royal Highness, we recommend you bring in dogs, because cats don't like dogs.'

The general was summoned and ordered to round up all the dogs in the kingdom and bring them to the palace.

Soon the cats were replaced by dogs. Now there was nothing but barking, and the dogs were a little less discrete with their personal habits.

It was time for another meeting and this time it was decided that as dogs were afraid of tigers, the kingdom's tigers should be rounded up and brought to the palace.

Soon the dogs started to disappear and the palace began to fill up with tigers.

This posed a serious problem!

The tigers were not only ferocious, but no one dared move a muscle, afraid that the tigers might attack them.

With great difficulty, another meeting was convened and it was decided that elephants be immediately summoned to the palace, because tigers were afraid of elephants.

No sooner had the elephants started to arrive than the tigers fled, leaving things in a bigger mess than before. Now the whole palace was full of elephants and there was no place to move.

The elephants were breaking things and the disaster was absolutely intolerable.

Pretty soon the palace started to fill up with elephant dung. The stench was indescribable.

Well, it was time for another meeting and this time it was decided that mice should be called in, because elephants were afraid of mice.

The general complied and as the mice started to arrive, the elephants left. Everyone at the palace found themselves back where they started, with mice everywhere.

The king now realised that he was actually to blame for the whole fiasco. Had it not been for his greed this would never have happened.

When a problem arises, people tend to look for immediate relief, but we often don't think about the fundamental solutions to the problems we face. When we fail to understand the true nature of the problem at hand, all too often we create even bigger problems with our short-term solutions. This ends up wasting our time and wastes precious resources.

What are the root causes of the problems you are facing right now in your life?

Thankfulness

Your journey of life began with your first breath.
Since then, the coming and
going of this breath has not stopped.
It will be with you throughout this life,
right until the last moment.
Be thankful that you are alive.
Appreciate this existence.

Breath brings you life.

Each breath, as it comes, is a true gift.

Pay attention to it as it comes into you.

When you can feel your own breath ushering in life,

it brings a comfort and a fulfilment.

If you ever feel small and insignificant, remember this miracle of breath happening inside you. With your effort, remembering the breath and being thankful for it can become a habit. Don't let anything else come in between you and your gratitude for this life. If there is conflict inside you, put an end to it. Focus on the simple joy of being alive, the simple gift of breath. A little effort towards that can bring a beautiful clarity and renew your passion for life.

You have an amazing ability to feel gratitude.

Not the gratitude you feel when someone opens a door for you and you say, 'Thank you.'

That is one kind of gratitude, but there is another.

When your ability to feel gratitude is tuned in to your existence, to the coming and going of your breath, it produces a unique kind of gratitude.

When you understand your ability to feel, your ability to find answers within you, your ability to be fulfilled, then gratitude wells up from within you.

Our ability to feel gratitude does not need to be improved upon.

It needs to be accepted as one of the most incredible powers we have.

There are many people who think, 'I need that. If only I had that, I would be happy.'
Very few think, 'I am happy because I am alive right now.'
If you don't understand that being alive itself is a source of happiness, then it doesn't matter how much you know, you are still missing a key piece of the puzzle.

What you are looking for is inside you.
All the answers you are looking for are
already within you.

The old man's milk

There was a wealthy old man who liked to drink a glass of warm milk before he went to sleep. Every night his servant prepared some milk and served it to the old man in his bedroom.

And every night the servant thought about how tasty it looked.

One day he decided to drink a quarter of the milk and replace it with warm water.

When the old man drank the milk, he thought to himself, 'Something is wrong. This tastes watery. Maybe my servant is tricking me.'

So the old man hired a second servant to keep an eye on the first servant.

In the evening, as was now his custom, the first servant made the milk and took out a quarter for himself.

When the second servant saw this he said, 'What about me? The boss hired me to keep an eye on you, but I won't say anything if you give me a quarter of the milk too.'

That night the old man's milk tasted even worse.

So he hired another servant to keep an eye on the first two. When the two servants took their share, the third servant said, 'Hey guys, what about me? I will keep quiet if you share the milk with me too.'

That night the old man's milk was three quarters warm water and one quarter milk. The old man was angry, so he hired one more servant and gave him strict orders to watch over the other three.

That night the three servants took their quarter and the fourth said, 'What about me?'

But the others said, 'If you take a quarter, then there won't be any left for the old man.'

The fourth servant said, 'Don't worry I have an idea.'

That night the old man waited in his bed, but his milk never came. Eventually he fell asleep. Then the fourth servant snuck into his room, took some foam from the bottom of the empty glass of milk, and gently put it around the old man's mouth.

When the old man woke up in the morning he was furious. He called all four servants.

'I am paying the four of you to bring me a glass of warm milk before bed and you are stealing my milk. You never brought my milk last night.'

'We did bring your milk, sire,' said the servants. 'Believe us. Go take a look in the mirror.'

The old man went to the bathroom and looked in the mirror. Sure enough, there was foam around his mouth, and the man thought, 'Maybe I did drink my milk last night.'

Real happiness and gratitude are feelings that well up from within. They are not dependent on external events such as belonging to a successful company or owning a lovely house. Having such things is fine, but happiness and gratitude don't follow a formula. Don't be like the old man in the story and fall for an external facade. When the gratitude can be felt inside you, you know it's real. And you know it's precious to you.

When you are touched by something, it connects you with a feeling of gratitude. When you can feel gratitude, it sparks your passion for life. When you have that passion within you, it allows you to feel compassion for others and you evolve. Being touched, feeling gratitude and experiencing passion for life, brings compassion and growth.

These things you can experience, they can become familiar to you.

If you can accomplish this, then doubt, hatred and anger will become strangers to you.

Seeds

Everything in your life begins with you sowing seeds.
Which seeds do you want to sow?

When we come into this life we are given seeds. There is the seed of kindness and the seed of anger. Love, under-standing, doubt and confusion are all seeds we have been given. Depending on which seeds we sow in the earth of this life, will be those trees we see in our garden. Some have beautiful flowers and others have a sticky, unpleasant sap. They all start out as little seeds, but as they sprout and grow they manifest their particular characteristics. Some we will like and others we won't.

It is up to you which seeds you plant and nurture in your life.

The archer and the oil salesman

In times gone by, some people used to make their living going from one village to another, earning a meagre amount from trading or performing for the public.

One such person was an archer. From a young age he had practised archery and had become good at it. He would travel and perform at fairs or for groups of villagers for whom any kind of entertainment was a welcome diversion.

The archer would set up a small target and then proceed to exhibit his mastery with the bow and arrow, splitting the arrows already embedded in the centre of the target. The villagers found all his displays entertaining.

The gathered people would applaud and encourage him to perform more of his seemingly impossible feats.

This went on, month after month, year after year. Not only did the archer earn quite a reputation for being a capable marksmen, but he also began to develop an inflated opinion of himself.

Then one day, while exhibiting his skills at a local fair, something unexpected happened.

A huge crowd had gathered to watch the archer showing off his skills. The crowd applauded and cheered him. But as the applause faded, he heard a faint voice from the back of the crowd saying, 'Ah, it's only a matter of practice.'

'Some fool making comments,' he thought to himself as he refocused for another shot, which was followed by cheers and applause, and then by the same irritating comment, 'Ah, it's only a matter of practice.'

Again he refocused and continued to impress his audience.

However, thoroughly agitated, he ended his show early and went looking for the man who had been making these infuriating comments.

At the back of the crowd he noticed an oil salesman sitting next to his two barrels of oil and a bunch of empty bottles.

'Hey you, are you the one who keeps saying it's just a matter of practice?' the archer demanded.

'Yes, that was me,' answered the salesman.

'What do you mean it's only a matter of practice? Don't you know I am the best? There is no one better than me. There is no one else with the same skills as me.'

'Don't be angry,' said the salesman. 'Because you practised you have become good. If you hadn't practised you would not be as good.'

'If it was only a matter of practice then anyone could do this. But it's me who has these abilities,' the archer countered.

'Let me show you something,' the humble salesman said, as he pulled out a coin from his pocket. It was a coin with a hole in the centre. He put the coin on top of an empty bottle, picked up the bulky barrel of oil and began to pour it through the hole in the coin, straight into the bottle without spilling a drop.

He turned to the archer and said, 'Now you try this.'

The archer then realised that it indeed was a matter of practice, for there was no hope of him being able to do likewise. He looked at the salesman with an apologetic expression.

'Dear archer,' the salesman said. 'You practise archery every day and you are good at it. I practise pouring oil every day and I am good at that. It truly is a matter of practice.'

Some people spend a lot of their time feeling irritable.
Arguing with their family makes them irritable, being told off
by their boss – all kinds of things make them irritable.

The problem is that if you practise being irritable every day
you will become an expert at it. Whatever you do every day,
you will get good at.

If you practise understanding, you will become good at understanding, just as if you practise anger, then that becomes
the skill you are honing.

If we spend our time acting unconsciously, then it becomes
second nature.

What do you want to become good at in your life?

38

When the desert blooms

The desert is a forbidding place. It is dry and dusty, the land-scape barren and colourless. The wind blows and dries out the sand and soil. The relentless sun strips away what little mois-ture is left, baking the ground hard. In places, you would think nothing could survive, and there are no signs of life.

However, just below the surface are countless seeds waiting for a chance to grow. Waiting for the rain. Sometimes 10 years can pass without a drop. No sign of rain to come, no guarantee that it will ever arrive.

In such circumstances, it can't be easy to keep hope alive and wait patiently, but those seeds never give up hope.

They wait in a state of readiness so that as soon as that rain arrives they are prepared and they can sprout.

One day the clouds begin to gather and the moisture in the air starts to rise. The distant sound of thunder heralds the coming of rain.

With the rising moisture, a sweet perfume starts to emanate.

Then comes the first drop, followed by another, and pretty soon it's a downpour. The water seeps down into the soil and those seeds that have been waiting such a long time start to come to life. With every bit of energy they have, they begin to sprout and grow.

Soon the desert is covered in bright reds and blues and oranges, as the flowers put on a magnificent display. A desert in full bloom is a thing bursting with life and beauty.

The seeds don't squander the opportunity or make excuses.

They don't say, 'I thought the rain was going to come next week.'

They wait for their chance in a constant state of readiness.

We also have seeds patiently waiting for a chance to flourish. The seed of fulfilment, waiting for the rain of clarity. Waiting for you to make the decision to be fulfilled. If you can make that choice and start to act on it, then within you those dormant seeds will bring forth their splendour.

There is a sickness eating away at humanity. Once you get this sickness it is difficult to cure. It is the disease of unconsciousness, of living this life unconsciously.

All around the world I say to people, 'Freedom is inside you.'

I also speak about this freedom in prisons, to people we consider to be the least free.

What is freedom?

If you want to feel that freedom then you have to cure the disease of unconsciousness.

There is a cure, and it is understanding the value of your existence. Knowing its preciousness.

Then no matter where you are, you can feel the real freedom that exists inside you.

As strong as water

A river flows freely. It doesn't ask anyone where it should flow, but finds the course that suits it best. In that course it may come across a rock. The rock says to the water, 'I will not move. You go around me.' With humility the water replies, 'OK, I will change my course.' The rock thinks it has won, but the rock doesn't know the water's true strength.

The water has persistence. Little by little the water carves away the rock. In time the rock has moved and the water is flowing in its place.

The canyons give testimony to the strength of the water. With great humility the water does not give up. It keeps flowing and slowly wears down the rock. In the end it is the solid rock that yields to the gentle supple water.

That water turns the stubborn rock into sand and washes it away.

Find the dream that is the most important to you. That dream isn't to climb to the top of the world's highest mountain. That dream is to be fulfilled.

The heart overflowing with gratitude brings an incredible feeling of happiness.

When you understand and accept what is precious, it makes you feel good.

When you are not going back and forth between yesterday and tomorrow, and become firmly rooted in the moment called *now*, you feel good.

When your foundation is not built on theories or formulas or beliefs, but on the solid ground of knowing the inner self, you feel good.

When you know the greatest friend is always with you, inside you, that feels very good.

The most important thing in your life is to really feel good from inside.

Feel this life, be grateful and let your heart be full of joy. Then you will truly begin to live.

Relationships

How do we build good relationships with others?
This is an important topic and something
we all have an interest in.

This section is a collection of questions and answers from
Prem Rawat's speaking engagements around the world.

My wife of 10 years believes that I will never be able to change and she has left me. How can I show her and my family that I have really changed?

Prem Rawat: If you change just for them it won't work. The day you change for yourself, they will be there like bees on a flower.

What is amazing is that you have not given up on yourself, and that is what is going to allow you to transform your life.

Inmate taking part in the Peace Education Program, Hyderabad Prison, India (2014)

Is there such a thing as karma and does that have anything to do with why we are here in prison?

Prem Rawat: If you look at yourself today, and where you are, this is the result of your choices. It has nothing to do with your karma. I recently received this comment from another inmate: 'Now finally I am learning that it was my choice that got me in here and what I choose will get me out, and what I choose will keep me out.' But if you go to a spiritualist, he will say, 'It is because of your karma you are here.' If I am here because of my karma, then what choice do I have?

A human being always has choice. Always. We are going to be a product of what we choose. Living life requires that you are conscious and that you make conscious choices.

Mr Rawat, I have been working in my company for five years now and I don't get on well with my boss. I tend to get irritated a lot and I find it hard to stay calm and feel good within myself. How can I develop a better working relationship with my boss?

Prem Rawat: It might feel like your relationship with your boss is a source of stress and irritation, and perhaps it is, but there is another, more important element to consider: what is happening within you? When you are not fulfilled, any little thing can make you angry, but when you are fulfilled, in the exact same circumstances, you can just let it pass without getting bothered by it. So the most important element is to resolve the conflict inside you and build a peaceful relationship with *you*. From that platform you have a much better chance of achieving peaceful relationships with others. Also, anger is a natural human emotion that we all feel at times. But it's a problem if it starts to become your normal mode of operation. If you get angry every day, you are practising it, and you'll become an expert at getting angry.

I recommend you become an expert at feeling good within yourself. Little by little, every day, make a conscious effort and you will see a change.

Mother,
London, UK (2015)

My two-year-old son is always grabbing toys out of his play-mates' hands and sometimes pushes them around in order to get the toy he wants. I want to teach him to be peaceful and kind. What can I do?

Prem Rawat: Young children have the full palette of emotions and they will express all of them, including the more negative emotions like anger and greed. You cannot prevent young children from going through these different emotions and exploring them. They need to go through that process. All you can do is provide them with a good environment, your support and love. Given the right support, most kids will pass through these phases quite quickly and choose a more peaceful way of interacting with others. We cannot make that choice for them, but we can give them the best opportunity to make a good choice.

Father,
Sao Paulo, Brazil (2012)

What can I do to bring my family more happiness?

Prem Rawat: First of all you need to find the happiness within yourself. A happy dad is the best present you can give your family. On top of that, if you want to make them happy, for five minutes, really listen to them. You want to give five minutes of paradise to your wife? For five minutes, just sit down and listen to her. It's the same for your kids, and indeed for anyone. Really listening to someone is something we often forget to do.

High school student,
Johannesburg, South Africa (2014)

I recently had an argument with a friend and exchanged some unpleasant words that I wish I hadn't said. How can we avoid these kinds of arguments and problems?

Prem Rawat: When I say a word, it comes out of my mouth. Then time grabs it and moves it, and now I can't touch it. I can't delete it, nor can I edit or change it. Every action I do, time will take it, grab it and move it. Now I have no control over it. That's why it requires an effort every day, to be aware of what I say, what I do, what I understand, what I accept, what I reject. It is an effort. I'm not saying I have mastered that, because it is not an issue of mastering it. It is an issue of making that effort continuously. Who has mastered drinking water? Nobody can say they have mastered drinking water and they don't need to drink it anymore. You get thirsty every day and every day you must drink water. Consciousness is exactly that. Awareness is exactly that. Every day, every moment, practise being aware.

Young woman,
eating disorder clinic, Palermo, Sicily, Italy (2015)

Is it possible to feel peace through affectionate human relationships?

Prem Rawat: First be whole with yourself, otherwise you can't have a truly successful relationship. When you are strong in yourself then you will be a good partner, a good friend, a good mother. In relationships we lean on each other. There are times when we need that support. It is like a chair you sit in when you can't hold yourself up. But if that chair is weak it won't support you. It will break and you will fall flat on the ground. When two individuals have their own inner strength, they can lean on each other and they will be there for each other when they have a rough patch in life. But if you are weak on the inside, your relationships are more likely to fail.

Elderly woman,
eating disorder clinic, Palermo, Sicily, Italy (2015)

What do you love and what do you fear in life?

Prem Rawat: I love life. I am fascinated that it changes and if I shape it right it evolves. With each day another gift is given, another flower opens.

I have fears too, lots of them. When I fly, as a pilot I am responsible for the lives of everyone on that plane. I am worried about the condition of the plane, the weather, the fuel.

I am afraid of lots of things. But I don't have to leave the fear as fear. I can take that fear and do something about it. Fear can either help you or disable you. You can take that fear and change it with your actions, your preparations. You can take steps to ensure that what you fear won't materialise. Your awareness and practical effort is needed. Living life consciously takes a lot of energy, but that is also when it becomes fun.

University student,
Barcelona, Spain (2015)

I was wondering, did it ever happen to you that you had bad times, when the problems just never seemed to stop?

Prem Rawat: Of course I have had times like that. I am a human being. I have had problems it seemed I would never get out of. When the problems come they appear huge, as big as the world. But I try to remember something. My problems are only as big as the space between my ears. They only exist inside this little box we call a cranium. That's as big as they can get.

Most of the time my choices get me into the problems, and my choices can get me out.

This breath is coming into you and every time it does, do you know what it is saying to you? The most powerful thing, this breath, is saying, 'Go, move, transform, live, exist.'

High school student,
Mazara del Vallo, Sicily, Italy (2011)

Why do the presidents and leaders involve the people in their disputes? Why can't they just sit down and talk without ruining people's lives?

Prem Rawat: A long time ago it was the king, in front of his troops, leading them into battle. So negotiations were of utmost importance because no one wanted to get killed. Today the leaders sit in a safe place while they send other people to go and fight. War should not even be an option. To kill another person for your own reasons, should not be accepted.

I would like to know more about how this message could be applied in the corporate world?

Prem Rawat: There is a fundamental problem with corporate structure. A human being has dreams, objectives he would like to accomplish. The only way he can do this is to have money so he can pay for accommodation, food, a car. So he gets a job. The company says, 'Work for us, and we will give you money and with that money you can do whatever you want.' This is how it starts. But the company has its own objectives, and soon says to the person, 'Fulfil our dreams, our goals, not yours.' This person now has no time for himself. Pretty soon, he gives up. What does he give up on? His dreams, his aspirations. As a result, he is not compatible with society, family or, friends, and the biggest problem, he is not compatible with himself. Peace has gone, dreams have gone. Now he looks forward to retirement. It's sad. However, the success of a corporation depends on individuals whose batteries are not dead. This message focuses on the battery and when that battery is fully charged, it brings a tremendous benefit.

Company President: Can you say a little more about these benefits?

Prem Rawat: People who are flourishing as individuals tend to be more flexible and have a greater capacity to evolve and take in new ideas and information. People who are stressed and frustrated in their daily lives tend to have little capacity to evolve and absorb new ideas. They are at their limit just trying to cope. Content human beings are creative. Innovation in business comes from individuals who are flourishing. Most people approach a problem with preconceived ideas of how it should be done. When the batteries are charged, however, people have the ability to look at the same problem from a totally new angle. This message can make a person feel full, restore creativity, enthusiasm, peace. And of course the corporation will do well when the people who work within it do well. This same principle applies to any group of people working towards a common goal. That group could be a company, a sports team, a school, even a family. When individuals flourish, it brings tremendous benefits to everyone.

About
Prem Rawat

For many years Prem Rawat
has been travelling and talking to people.
This section is an insight into his life and work.

A lifetime dedicated to sharing a universal message all around the world.

Prem Rawat was born in a small northern Indian village on the outskirts of Haridwar in 1957. His father, Sri Hans Ji Maharaji, was a renowned speaker on the topics of inner peace and fulfilment. Prem learned much from his father and was encouraged by him to develop his natural talent as a speaker. When Prem was just eight years old, his father passed away and Prem took on the responsibility of continuing his father's work. He began travelling and speaking at events during his school holidays and many people were touched to see a child speak so simply and clearly on such a deep topic.

In 1971, at age 13, he made his first trip out of India when he was invited to speak in London, England, and in Los Angeles in the United States. Since that first trip Prem has spent over 40 years travelling around the world speaking in more than 250 cities and addressing live audiences totalling over 15 million people.

His addresses have been translated into 75 languages and his audiences range from intimate gatherings to events with hundreds of thousands of people. In one event in Bihar,

India, approximately 500,000 people gathered to hear him speak.

What Prem talks about is simple and universal. 'Within all people lies an inherent thirst to be content.' Crossing the barriers of culture, religion, economics, politics, education and social status, from inmates in prisons to people in war-torn regions of the world, he brings the same message to people from all walks of life.

Prem's work has been acknowledged by governments and civil groups around the world. He has been invited to speak at such venues as Kensington Palace in the UK, the EU parliament and the Italian, Argentinian and New Zealand parliaments. He has also been invited to speak at prisons, forums and prestigious universities around the world.

In November 2011, a special event entitled 'Peace and Wellbeing in the European Union' was hosted by the First Vice-President of the EU parliament, Gianni Pittella. Prem Rawat was the keynote speaker. The event was attended by a large international delegation of politicians and VIPs representing institutions interested in peace from around the EU.

As a direct result of the inspiration of Prem's message, the first ever Peace Declaration was signed at the EU parliament.

In 2012 in Malaysia, at an award ceremony titled '7 Billion

Reasons for Peace', Prem Rawat received the BrandLaureate lifetime achievement award. Previous recipients of this award include Hillary Clinton and Nelson Mandela.

Speaking before an audience of 130,000 people at Jawaharlal Nehru Stadium, New Delhi, India, 2003

Speaking at the commemoration of the 60th anniversary of the United Nations held in San Francisco, USA, 2005

Speaking at the 'Peace and Well-being' event in the European Union alongside the First Vice-President of the European parliament, Hon. Gianni Pittella, Brussels, 2011

The Prem Rawat Foundation (TPRF)

As well as his speaking engagements, Prem has also started a charitable foundation to help people live with dignity, peace and prosperity. One of the foundation's projects, called *Food for People*, started when Prem visited Bantoli in India. The children of the region, though rich in spirit, were grossly malnourished. Working with the local community, the foundation built a facility that provides a daily meal and clean water to those who need it. The facility provides long-term support to the community and is now run by local people with the help of the foundation. This has had a dramatic impact, decreasing crime rates in the region. Due to better nutrition the first children from the region are now attending university.

There are also Food for People facilities in Ghana and Kathmandu, Nepal, with more being planned. The programme puts great emphasis on respecting the dignity of the recipients and their culture. The foundation works with the recipients to ensure poverty can be tackled at a fundamental level, so that the local people can ultimately become fully self-sufficient.

The Prem Rawat Foundation also provides contributions to disaster relief, working alongside other major charities

Answering questions from inmates in Zonderwater prison, South Africa, 2014

Prem Rawat Foundation 'Food for People' facilities in Otinbi, Ghana (left) and Tasarpu, Nepal (right)

around the world.

Another aspect of the foundation's work is the Peace Education Program, a series of DVDs combined with opportunities for reflection and discussion on various key topics such as strength, choice, hope and personal peace. The course has been presented in 48 countries by a large variety of organisations and community groups, including colleges, youth programmes, adult education programmes, hospice centres, retiree centres, prisons and parole rehabilitation programmes. In prisons, the programme has been linked with reducing violent activity and falling reoffending rates. One prison guard at the Dominguez jail in San Antonio, USA, said, 'Almost four years later the programme is still turning out good offenders that have gone back out into society and do not return to the Dominguez unit. The behaviour of those who attend the programme has noticeably improved and their disciplinary record has gone way down, if not totally.'

A father of four and keen photographer

When not busy travelling around the world, Prem gets to spend time relaxing with his family or pursuing some of his many hobbies. Prem enjoys painting, making music and photography. His eldest daughter, Wadi, says, 'My father is incredibly kind, good humoured and funny. He always makes us laugh. When we were younger he would tell us fantastic bedtime stories. He is very dedicated, both to his family and his work. I have learnt from watching him that if you remain clear, make good choices and maintain a consistent effort you can accomplish a lot.'

Prem with his grandson

Contents

Splitting the Arrow

Understanding the Business of Life

1st Edition release date December 23rd 2015
2nd Edition release date February 18th 2016
3rd Edition release date June 7th 2016

Author **Prem Rawat**

Illustrations   Aya Shiroi

Editors   Max Whittle
Michiyo Kotani
Adharanand Finn

Publishing   Bunya publishing corporation, LLC
President Yutaka Kinoshita

Prem Rawat's official representative for Japan

45 Iida, Obuse-machi, Kamitakai-gun, Nagano Japan
http://www.premrawat-japan.com/en

Design   Takeshi Shindo

Production assistance   Paul Bloomfield
Takashi Yokosato
Chizuko Nakamura
Miho Hattori
Shugo Tsumura

Printing   TONIC S.A., Athens, Greece